PRIMITIVE AWE

MIRIAM E.WALSH

BOOK 2: RANDOM SERIES

ardornata
publishing

Cover art by Miriam E. Walsh
Book design by Miriam E. Walsh

ISBN 978-0-9836598-1-5

ardornata publishing
www.ardornatadesign.com

TABLE OF CONTENTS

About The Author

Miriam E. Walsh has worn many hats to pay the bills:
mental health worker at a detox unit, drafter in the engineering field
and graphic designer --- but she has always donned the hat of a
poet.

For many years, at her home on the south shore in Massachusetts,
she has tended to many writing projects, the culmination of which
is the Random Series of books. These poems have been written in
many places; lunch breaks, poetry readings, train rides and, yes,
car rides!

She has been published in U.M.Ph.! Prose Online and is a regular
fixture at local poetry venues including "Poetry: The Art Of Words
Mike Amado Memorial Series" in Plymouth, Massachusetts.

Miriam E. Walsh has an BS Degree in Psychology from
Bridgewater State College, where she also minored in art. She is
an accomplished photographer/visual artist and a member of the
Plymouth Arts Guild.

random series
book 1 : beautifully alien refraction
book 2 : primitive awe
book 3 : forced continuity
book 4 : small lucidities

dulcet 03

you swallowed down
your self-evaluated fate
like
sugared strawberries;
popping them into
your mouth
and slowly noticing
every texture of seed,
every granule of sweet,

before sliding it
down your throat.

you didn't even hesitate
to think
to choke
upon it.

a child
accepting the inevitability
of the argument
in the next room,
but finally knowing
that the noise
could not bruise her.

the pain
that glistened
with your eyes
was a love
you simply decided to have,

as you spoke
frankly
of all the things
you never would.

and the stars
finally breathed clearly
above us;
the cold releasing its
constriction
and they would flicker
for the air
had finally thawed.

you licked your lips,
still tasting
the even now
dissolving confection
on your tongue.

your gaze
washing it down
with a drink of sky,
blinking as if upon
a million
freed fireflies,
your voice
whispered with the
caring fear
of making them scatter.

"I never know
what to do with myself
when beauty
finally comes . . ."

beautiful ones 03

the ones
left allowed
to have a soul.
the intelligent eyes,
the willingness
to die
if that
simple configuration
of a gaze
is ever asked to.

the sufferers
calloused for survival,
the comfortable,
the quiet panic of
the never tested;
these brittle forms
turn to dust
when their bones do.

and when even the
dust forgets itself.

but these ones,
these are memories
that so remind us
of ourselves
that they are
the archetypes
of all we aspired to
as children
and grieved for
when we would never be.

the beautiful ones.

and all these
as
children
are to us.

a next to last word 03

a shade
of burgundy hair
in the pattern
of form
and thought
spilling from
the pen.

it reminds me
of who you loved
instead of me.

and now
at this distance,

a woman
looking upon this child;
I understand
why.

but now
I do not understand
why she loved you. .

negative space 03

nothing
with more meaning,
emptiness
with more depth.

it is
the 0 holding the 1,
the sky carving
the mountain,
the pause before a note,
the silence
that defines the word,

the expanse that makes
the universe,

the black.

nothing
is in
everything;
in anything
that was ever
something.

cicatrix 03

with always
a claw to my coitus
all creatures
born from me
begin with scars.

it is the scraped skin
the lacerated,
excavated
depth of a bleeding
that might be words,
that might be silence,
that just may be
the why? and the what?
behind
my long-lidded
stare
intothroughbeyond
you.

and
even with
your polished finger

there

as if
poking upon
a road-side kill,
as if blaming
with the skill
of all cowards;

this well has
only a long hidden
corpse for you,
only this black milk
to drink from.

you attempt
to neuter me;
an exit wound
rather than
an entrance.

a scar
has only one sense,

memory.

dire Boolean 03

she sat
a disaster
of folded hands

the very
enmeshed
and
organized pattern
of just before
collapse.
as if it
would pass
if she
held her breath,
glazed her eyes;

as if she faded
enough in those
moments
for it to not see
her.

the only thing
she smiled
upon

was my reluctance
to leave.

"I can take
myself
when I want. . .
hands and eyes
are not what
stops me. . . "

she called it
cowardice.
this quiet will,
this long breath
braided
with both
sigh and silence.

"it's cowardice
not to
when it's the
only thing left to do. .
. . just a choice."

a fractured fractal
of twitches
upon her upper lip
reflected down into
the words
she wasn't saying,
but managed a form
even to my
clumsy perception
when her
swollen eyes
squinted upon
a light
with its distance.

and the code
of twitches stopped
all words dissolved
to a fluttered awe

and she was
unreachable.

I left her
in her folded hands.

ptsd 03

I protect my breath
with the strangle
of my hands.

the sound of this
is a insect
ruthlessly
making a home
for its progeny
upon the edges
and folds
of my thought.
its mindless
will
will not
leave my mind.

my name is
a pulse
of two beats
and a weak
tremble between

it is a cold terror
that follows me
into the morning
and no longer
is satisfied
with the corners
of my peripheral eye

but as a creature
curl- spined
and feeding
in this non-visible
place
within my ribs.

it makes me
breathe hard

and I can feel
every point
just above
and a little
forward
of my ear:

an exit wound
scratching
a rampage
from within
my throat.

my teeth clench
into a cage
for it.

rainforest 03

there was a rain forest
creeping
upon the leaves
around me,
walking with
miiiiiiiiiiiiiiiiiiiiiiiillipede feet
texturing
the night
and its many grey
patchworks
of silences.

the mosses
curled
and rose,
a lifted tangle of arms
raising me
shimmering,
raining upon me
an ambient,
ambivalent moon
ensnared in
black branches.

the scent of dying
flowered upon
my nostrils,
sweet and stinging
each nerve ending
with its recollections
in a maudlin mist.

a molecular mesh
twisting my limbs

in this place
of extinction.

and in this death
i am at elevations;
a black mountain
that arches the sky
with the gravity
of its void,

trapped upon
its foot
in tidal pools small
enough
for my understanding,
waded all things
unfamiliar,
waiting for names
from an
inexperienced tongue.

far from homes
at depths clinging
to the roots of trees
that are but
unrelated islands to me.

here I can see
the rain forming,
its opaque whisper
attempts to inundate
that which swims

but the birds
drown it
with a symphonic
sense of ocean.

persephone 03

I have been
destroyed,
barren
but bearing
the dry scream
of still born birth.

when I wake
when I dream,

between
I sleep

trying to find
a place
between
seeking and surviving.

this seed
I have swallowed
has contours cutting
the delicacy
of my throat
of my willingness
to accept,
believe.

and closed upon,
this breath waits
as does
the air
without
for communion
in my voice.

a word,
a remembered,
I am choking upon.

I am a season
between
the frozen sun
and
the fiery moon.

driven philosophy 03

there were rhythms
even to her
annoyance.

her mouth
strummed
and
clicked
a sinew
of gum
like an improvisational
music.

it was jazz
to the rant
that sang
mistimed & mistuned
spilling
over her teeth
by the tongue
casually punishing
the air
with the
epithets & epilogue
of lectures
of how
there were
"far-too-many-people"
in this world,

that it was
a flaw
of civilization
of how we became
too good at staying
alive & killing
everything else.

but she loved
and would not go
without her fossil-burner.

she whipped
around corners
with the same
brusque articulation
of her words.

maneuvering
the Pontiac
with the ferocious
territoriality,
even in the midst
of an impromptu
sermon
of how humans
were not predators
that only
dictatorssociopaths-
and-
writersofconservativepolicy
wanted to believe
we were
to win
all their arguments,

but we were just
monkeys mimicking wolves
a prey conquering
predator
through costume
like a shaman.

brakeless
she swooped
a hawk
down the curve
of a will,
throwing back
her head as the
speedometer
twirled like a compass
in the Bermuda Triangle.

but stopped
in panicked squeal
for two yellow
frozen eyes
in the road.

apsis 03

you catch me
with the
hook and curve
of your
architecture

and the arches
of balconies
tell me how
you know me

with
their shelter
and
their shadow.

with the way they
stop
me from
falling
into the sky
when i look
upon a star
that is no longer
there

and want to
follow
its path
into blackness;

fascinating me
to some place
closer to earth

and still
raise me
just a little
closer to
the moon.

agnostic gnowing 03

you asked me
that if I was
so dissatisfied
with god
where would I be,
where would I look
when I died
but into its eyes.

I closed and
looked into my own,

and I was sun
warming a glittering white sand;
and then I was sand
cradling a black swarming ocean;
and then I was ocean
driving the pulse of a wind;
and then I was wind
my every invisible inch of skin
curling upon your hair
and then . . .

and then
you touched my hand
and I
answered only
with my eyes
yours.

trespasser 03

honest fingers
on a my back,
an empath
among vampires,
a stranger
feeling the lives
of seeming strangers.
recorder of patterns
of faces,
of pasts,
a trespasser
in a garden
who alone
can smell the fragrance
that the flowers
themselves
never know.

arms spread
upon the earth
to feel its hum,
a pulse
that silences
all others
with its magnitude
its age.
a skin
ever stimulated,
ever sensitive
but never desensitized
a passion
without a lover
to which
a voice is never
the mouth that speaks
but
growing back
into old shapes
into the raw crevices
in the muscles of
my throat

I know colors
of these blossoms
without my eyes

the small 03

I walked
within the wooded
sun,

the boughs bent
in remembrance,

as if inquiring
of the footsteps
of the castless shadow,
the mist
that dangled
just above a lip
in speaking;
present
always within my words
but
beyond my explanation

a dragonfly
sunning
its wings,
the wind
rhythmic dance
of white flowered
weeds,
the afternoon
still
moist heavy
upon the skin;

the morning
still upon the eyes,
a shelter
among
small leaves

a hope
that foams
somehow
filling more
than it is;
a voice
of imperfect tones
that somehow
the ear
hears better.

in my short attention
span
eons pass more
quickly than
they did
eons ago.

making me
god
to this small.

and god
small
to me.

I need
a cataclysm
to humble me
or
maybe
just the view
where I
cannot see it.

inheritance 03

from where comes
the jar
that holds these scrolls?

excavated
cracked
but lovingly repaired
this consecrated
concentrated effort
is wasted upon
a shape
that is unrelated
to its content.

a scripture
that had no promise
other than the
far-focused gaze
of two gauze glowing
oceaned moons
that hung above
the serene horizon
of your parted lips.

your words
were wind
and could with a touch,
innumerable and invisible,
cast aside the strands
of my hair.

I was a prophet
until
I believed my own
predictions,

feeling the shroud
that was your skin
my fingertips;
why do you have me
read this book
when there is so much
dust upon it?

it is to pull me back,
it is to infect me
with possession,
that faded poison
in the penmanship
of an unapprenticed
hand of a school girl poet.
can I shape myself,
into the shape of your youth

you have no thought
but to steal
from me.
my desperation

even as I age

is to be
my only inheritance.

eros of thanatos 03

this desire is
too complete,
too devout,
too much
in worship
of a knowing
to play
with an
unknowing.

and the spring sun
reminds me
and the warm air refuses
to be kind to me,

warming
places I made
frostbitten,
resuscitating
that which should
be left dead
because their amnesia
of me
makes them intangible
for me anyway.

I am picking upon
a wound again,
licking upon this cut
just to feel it,
just to taste it,
just to have a feeling,
just to bleed
and make sure my heart
is still beating

a pain,
my ribs tightening,
the throat twisting,
galvanized
heated and harpooned
but does not penetrate
completely.

this hard skin
is brittle in its rigidity.
it cracks,
even earth
has her inner rumblings
her occasional bouts
of self destruction,

and I too am
a blue
holding back an abyss,
a green,
growing over battlefields.
this rain washing away the
dust,
this wind carrying away a
storm.

to exist
as if it never happened
to glow
when it would be
too easy,
to grow dim,
to stop,
to disappear
to sleep.

clearly drunken 03

this drink
creates more interesting
patterns in me
than any drunkeness

your hands
spoke with
a child's language
a mimicry
that shaped the air
with its
sincere lunacy
of absence.
its pronounced
lineless imagery,
a pantomime
with all the hidden
of a hexagram.

the flicker of your
eye;
spoke binary
to the satellites
orbiting you
with their flattery.

your gestures
betrayed the secrets
of all surrounding
as they giggled
your strategic foolishness.

and how drunk
you were
upon their spirits

then suddenly,
you bellowed,
a laugh
that shattered
chandeliers
and gave echoes
skins
to shove with,
pushing
the wine sipping
insipid
whines
to the wall
with the fear
that you might
spill upon them,

though secretly
they were thirsty

conspicui 03

voices
of a distant flute,
the blue sky
of that summer
that only the
star remembers
and my transient
mortal mind is
a dusk
with a texture
that anticipated calm.
and here am I

conspicui.

it hurts too much,
it hurts too little.

this alien flesh
that understands
the expansive sigh
of adorning night
more than the human
adoring eye.

still in my ear
a trickling of crickets
and the fingertip warmth
of a hesitating firefly.
an unknown
architecture
within my
messageless eyes
I am a new form
of megalith.
my color
that of suns;
a new sky
with my silence.
cataclysm
has already fallen
and my
history
is of an unrecorded
civilization.

gods will not
convert me
with punishment,
man will not
have me
with his lies.

feral 03

this sun
it makes my sights
breathe for me

with all the blue
I am breathing.

the primal primitive
rounding
of a word
upon a lip.

when my body
has lost
the sequence
to do so.

a finger
lightly
upon my brow.

forcing outward
my teeth
passed the origins
of a smile
and
a muscle flinch
away from a threat.

voice I cast,
upon the sky
this throat
launches
a bird,
a flight,
that pulls me with it.

an then closed
with a sudden
punctuation,
a closing;
an angry woman
upon a lover.

only my toes
mother me
with a sense
of earth.

there were times
when such a place
was earned

so I may
close my eyes
and pretend
that I do not
need it.

and still is
with the flit of a feather
and a show of color.

if only we
were treated
as animals.

but
my lungs
are too
buoyant

the waiting 03

the trauma
is not
in the gun
but in the wanting

the only touch
that will soothe
the relentless
itch
just behind
my eye,

the doubt.

this will scare
these hands from
my throat,
so I can
breathe
just a while.

dull-eyed
and stoned
with spent fury
staring
at the air
waiting for
a vision
that must come
with such
insanity.

but
a panicking animal,
I have
flailed to hard

and there are
too many
resulting turbulences
surrounding.

so that
the calm
must come

from the waiting.

unsounded 03

the barely heard
sound of rising;
mourning note
that repeats
to gentle comfort
tenderness of your voice.
it reminds me
of my heartbeat,
an undeveloped
fetal stirring
waiting to be born,
dreaming
as a bubble clasped,

my brain
rapidly depressurized
slowly, seeping
consciousness
to sustain
equilibrium
to oblivion.

my lids
came down.
my eyes adapted
to the darkness
but
I dilated like
a pupil
into black.

into this submergence
I sunk.

unsounded

ephemerid 03

my lips
are numbing
upon a sweetness
and my eyes
are searching
for orion,
a memory
for which the
pyramids
were built,
a hope
for which
telescopes
pray.

and in the grass
insects
are transmitting
signals
to a disproved
god
with a chord
of relentless zeal;
an unquestioning
that might just
conjure
a deity
from a void.

unknowing
that the stars
do not wait for us.

or perhaps
knowing
just that.

white trash war   03

you slap me
a precise
measure
of your tether

and perhaps
in my own
self hatred
I make you
my personal
atrocity
so that there is
a reason
for all the
tears I wanted
to cry,
so I can convince
myself
that my failure
was unavoidable.

and I hold you
here
with these
pink soaked eyes
until you've hit me
so many times
that you join me
here
and your legacy
is nothing more
than a red stain
opposite
the shotgun
you place between
your own teeth.

enemy 03

your fingers,
an anemone
in worship

but I only saw
an enemy.

i washed
my face
with the air;
something for my hands
to do
something
to feel,
to pass
this unpassable moment.

ostracized
from my
own skin.

you expect me
to respond to touch.

I cannot

all my reflexes
are hurting ones,
all my responses
are practiced.

the careful breath,
the casually precise eye
blink,
staring just behind you;
all my ache
clinging to a
rare annunciated tongue.

I am too used to living here
just outside home,

just far away
enough
to miss both of us.

inward   03

...a fold of inward,,
an atom excessing itself

rupturing
into these astral firefiles
this night
simmering cimmerian.
the first day
is effervescing
in the creation
of the first suns.

a fabric pierced,

an embryonic membrane,
a microbe
mother to macrocosm.

there are lives
in the curves
of my fingertips

all this shape
a cross-section
of a molecule
whose bonds are only
visible as time.
swimming in the viscous,
a plankton
glowing in the black
of a volcanic trench
deep below
the star of another sky.

its sea,
a spray sparkling
and each refracting
liquid crystal,

a fold of inward . . .

venerate 03

two
so convinced
of each others insanity
that we are
one
fear.

you saw me
brilliant;
just then
I was sure
you had no eyes,
that somehow
you had mistaken
my
idle thought
for
an idol
to light your candles to.
the warm wax
hardened
upon my feet,
a translucent shell
of your
immaculate
expectation
attempting
to make me a statue
for your worship

even your
words
hooked upon the walls
with its
edges and curves
as if the wind
would disperse them
and leave them
strewn as ants
upon the pavement.
subjugating
their meaning
to the formic
uniformity,
a form
suspended by
habit
rather than
inhabitation,

offering them
as mindless
extensions
of my intention
and even as
every time
you reached for me
still
your fingers
scattered back
from the abruptness
of what I might do,

as if trying to
alight
to a place of safety.

reckoning   03

I am
trying to invent
a new emotion
to replace
how I felt for you.

a new architecture
that does not know
your echo
but traps it
making it mute
with its acoustics

a fold just before
reaching me,

before brushing
each hair upward
so it stands;
a million mayan priests
arms up
with an offering
for the sun
that is really a comet
ever-filling the sky
fulfilling
its destructive destination
with me.

I have burned off
my atmosphere
so I can breathe
in one
ocean swell
of a scream,
in one
electromagnetic pulse
of willful
non-motion.

break   03

unmitigated,
uncircumnavigated
intent,

as a child
you believed in god
but it did not
believe
enough in you
to exist,

and even
at this very human
moment
you did not worry on
where you were
going
but were happy to
surrender this
shell,

a hand
that did not
know your impulse
a skin that would not
stretch
to your intention
wearing a flesh
that would not grow
nor has any
organ or sense
for that which
you know is real.

with only
your doubt
as proof.

I envied you
your obsessions.

the glint
that held your eyes
fixated.
the awe
that stole all expression
from your face
leaving a textureless
clarity
that would almost
reflect
and allow me
a glimpse
into that which only
you could see.

breaking

giving over
to the demand
of death
as if your body
did not matter
so sure you had
another form
awaiting you.

m 03

always around you
a music emerging,
a honey that glisten,d
savoring itself in
the higher childlike quavers
and
in an amber that settles
in its most rounded
of timbres,

but always a substance
that simmered like a spice
and surrounded like an incense,

you inundated
my senses

as if
constant & harmless
sin
was all that could
allow me
to breathe
in the privacy
it provided:
a song, a voice
dissolving into
mouth shaping
heart raping
elation.

and you said
that god created us

just in time to die

that this skin
was just
a bubbled off encasement
of a divine will
that peers into
a petri dish,
an indifferent
experimenter.

while we,
a raw rhythm
of heartbeats
fighting
the eventuality
of our own stillness

with each second,
with each savored.

in this torn caul
the battered edges
of self-awareness.

virgin 03

a hand in
curvature of
mocking
turned upward,
worshipping
as if weaving
the thread
of time

between
thumb & forefinger

drinking the sun
from the backs
of your eyes,
you tilted
your head
held back
as if trying to
saturate
your corners
with its forgetfulness

all so that you could
remember

well passed
the past,
you could recall;
a before time
when a clock
was a face
pursing its nose
at you
like an old woman
whose expression
you did not
understand
but could
ignore

a virgin bloodying
the grass,
some innocent
left,
leaving
the brittle hardening
of a cocoon.

vanities 03

your privacy
was a graying hair
upon your shoulder;
it curled
and trembled
against the darkness
of all others.

a piece of child
you outgrew
your mirrors,
your vanities,
for a reflection
for a world of larger ones;
your limbs
stretched and grew;
the height of your wanting,
the depth of your need.
you were soon
your own
antiquity.

an expectation
already filled
or
already failed upon.

a dream
too many times
woken within
and then forgotten.

a dust
too many times
disrupted.
a husk collapsing
forgetting the shape
of the life
it once held.

candlemas (imbolc) 03

pagan tree
in the night,
its lights
candles
of a separate sky,
stars
knowing another dark,
with their
untouching.

but knowing
a forgotten intimacy
with the sight
of each others distance.
the planets aligned
as the gleam,
as the intent
of your gaze.

forming
a constellation
of an entirely new
revelation.

one that finally
revels.

you danced,
a negative space
formed
by the emptiness,
by the sound
you floated upon,
and it held
you from sinking
when nothing else could.

even as
your eyes glow
scattered,
synchronized,
with the glittering
of notes
in the music
you found both
solace & grief in.

interrupt 03

and somehow
the sound of crickets
transcends,
silences you
until your face
has the wonder
of summer lightning
and pierces
the sky.
a storm
whose
rains drops
conspire
with the slow
firing of this neuron
to interrupt
my pen.

tao 03

"those who know
do not say,
and those who say
do not know"

all that is,
is god parting its lips
in what it is
about to say.

and will end
once it is
spoken.

and even this
is not true.

sfumato 03

*The blurring or softening of sharp
outlines in painting by subtle
and gradual blending of one tone
into another.
Italian sfumare, to evaporate,
Latin, to smoke.*

sfumato,
that face
formed clouds.

changeling
you cast
yourself
to the histories
of the lives surrounding.
a reservoir,
an ocean,
carrying in your eyes
a depth
that bled into
all others.

a calm of ecstasy,
a blinded insight.

a pulse of unsummoned
exertion.

hands upon glass
or the
smoke painted hands
in prehistoric caves;
a leaf,
seemed your divided
profile,
both
mother and lover
to yourself,
the distance you kept
made for a proximity,
arms length
from the horizon.

nova 03

a sun cut
from parchment
the veil is the
black
the illusion
is the distance
to which
the stars
are held.

and snow it falls
tracing with its
gentle fingers
each slender branch;
that would stir itself
with each tenuous tremor
of thought
into a decorative lace.

in fields of white
I know the blindness
of my being
as every prism facet.
it is
the sound of hollow
finding my ears,
as the depth
of darkened skies
finds my eyes

I am being told
a secret
from a nova
that has long died
and is resurrected
in this echo.

I shiver in its cold.
I am its flesh
and its last words
but my tongue
has failed its
articulation.

only my sigh
pronounces it
correctly

lumberer 03

an echo
that follows me
like a ripple
does the sound
of wind,
a lumberer
that expands
the hollow
of each doorway
with the groan
of protesting limbs.

my eyes are
fused closed
because I can see everything

before me

and all that i
have ever trespassed
has even fallen
short of sin.

if only, sliced open
and pulled down,
I could find a reflex
to accommodate
this dissection.

but only study
the shape
upon the wall
and impassively
regard the points
of these pins.

black milk 03

the rain
traveled
for me,
cratering the ground
with its
memory and grief
for sky.

the crack and rumble
of a life
somewhere emerging.

it growls
from hunger.
but I am far
enough away
to be vulnerable
only to the thought
of its teeth:

the clock striking
heard only in the sleep

of a mortals
intermittent depth of mind.

reminding the simian
in me
of similar times.
of floods,
of a frightening mother
that was only
asking me
to drink.

zealot 03

an amateur prophet,
your are imposing
upon me
a series
of emaciations,
of incantations
meant to transform
me.

but
immaculate
there is barely a scratch
in your words,
in your presence,
a hesitation
that allows for thought
as
my fingers wrestle
upon an unseen
knot;
not
knowing
when the furnace
will stop cooking
in my stomach.

and the bodies
upon it.

I am being fed
upon
by a that which
demands
that I be blissfully
unaware
of its teeth.

delusion
is a mantra
but
I have as many
words for consciousness
as Eskimos
have for snow.

arthritic 03

and such
an angelic face
and slender form.

outside
I am youth
I am a source
of arthritic hands
reaching back
from painted
wrinkled eyes
longing;
long
dark hair
soft upon my fingertips
should know
no
entanglement
and though
my joints
do not ache,
I know pain.
it is the lover
I imagine
and the empty
I wake up to.

love is myth
to the young,
and a warm memory
to the dying;
a voice that
peoples
the darkness.

oneiros 03

you hung
as if attached to
a string
but somehow
you still
managed to
enjoy your wings.

from the ground
I watched
you
fluttered & disturbed,
a moth
on a not quite
secure mountain
that was my knee,
a twitch
that was to
your sleep
an earthquake,
as the sky's
movement,
white outrunning blue,
was the smiling
of your
opening eyes.

solipsis 03

I saw
the ocean;
the shoulder of its tides
carrying back toward me
the burden;
the incarnations
I thought
long sunk
within it.

only my final voice
will make the journey,
a bubble
rising,
then opening itself
upon the surface
of a storm.

but I will
only be
a brief glistening
upon it
or a dark depth
carrying it.

always ending
stranded upon
a shore.

it is time to
dive back in.

hide 03

you told me
of a dream

a night
inside of me
from behind my eyes,
wearing my skin.

but it was not
to know me,
to feel what
this flesh felt.

only a disguise
to describe
and make manifest
all that you were
supposed to have,
supposed to be.

so subordinate
was my soul
to your schedules

that this pelt was
all you saw of me.
a thing to wear;

a casing
that held
and
never betrayed
all your acts
of injury.

a hide
for all that was hidden.

maya 03

a quantum
spattering
carving the floor
into an
indecipherable dynamic
of all that is
being dragged
across it.

its patina
is age,
is anonymity
that eventually
comes with it.
until it is an unknown
that attracts
those who already
know the
curve and line
of its language
but will not
admit it.

a perpetual
hide and seek
of philosophers
to keep themselves
in business.

river 03

I let it flower
in my chest
until its scent
is a drug
that fills my thoughts

with its nothing.
with its everything.

and I am
a river
that knows its own
source.

and I can
feel myself
uncaringly floating
through a night of
currents and rapids

and the lids
of my eyes
have become
a circle of sky
with only my stars
upon it.

the water
is warm.

and it has
all the fingers
of my mothers hands

pilgrim 03

banished
ostracized
outside my own boundary
extradited
into my own hands.

I am a
wounded pilgrim
upon an unfolding plain
of my homeland.
the uncurling scroll
of an unveiling plane.

and this bleeding
closes upon the night,
opens upon the sunrise.
both sun and moon
finding each other
in the eclipse of my eyes.
I am blinded
by all that was
hidden.

with my pain-lit eyes
I confront the sky
with my scars
even as my face
is just a ghost
of features
that the clouds
play upon,

but left
a corona,
the illumination
of its traces upon
my retina of infinite curve;
my breaths an infinity between.

I fold my hands
to my brow
as if there were
a map
in the lines
of my palms.

this 03

a rebellion
against the hope
imposed upon us.

it is a quiet honesty
that makes a cavern
of your throat
for all it wants to say;
complete
with its quiet
worshipping,
fire-lit paintings;
its primitive awe.

it is an empty
that holds a place
for that
which will never form.
a space that is
a memory
of a shape
it had imagined
and decided
remembering
will do just as well.

but it is also
acceptance.

a hollow
that breathes,
a grass
receiving snow.

and it is the
only place
where threat
has no echo.

like all things
in life,
merely a ritual
to forget dying

and daily prepare for it.

the stoning 03

in this room
of teeth wanting veins,
hollows wheezing for
wholes
and the sweet
unthought-of words
of chocolate- covered
abscesses.

you were the only
one
who did not know me.
but the only
one
to see me.

standing silently
within this stoning circle
your hands too clenched
to throw even
the weight
of an expectation
upon me.

but
the wait
was upon you.

my eyes ached
with the worlds
expanding within
them
so full
of desperate blindness
I was.

my mouth
a barely caught breath,
a word deciding to be unsaid;

for all the ears
present
were only gathering evidence.

scrape beneath
my fingertips
and they will
find only their own
flesh and blood.

faith 03

and I drifted
a levitation
in the waiting

if only I
had the faith
to lift my feet
from the ground

but I am tethered
from behind
my rib cage
from the organ
where
intelligent monkeys
pretend their
affections are,
to an earth
for all that
science admits
might well be
upon a turtles back,
and another . . .

a crucifix
tells me that
I will not suffer for nothing,
a round belly
laughs at
my insistence
that I suffer at all,

while every man
says they love me
while they stare at
my chest.

maybe they're
looking for my
affections there.

I am a planet
with a cycle of
extinctions.

closing my eyes
in my only resolve
as my creatures
are burned
from me.

I know the silence
of ashes
and how
too much upon
my hands
numbs
my fingertips,
dissolves
my fingerprints,

until there is
no trace,
no form
to touch the sky
for me.

and somehow
from this
dust
I must make
clay.

beacon '03

I had a dream of you,

treading to your ankles,
still oceans more.

still your arms raised
anticipating depths
that may suddenly rise
or
that you may sink into

as if keeping your hands dry
would keep you from drowning.

but it really only takes an inch.

it was a candle you held up.

to make translucent
the void
to make lucid
your eyes;

two rings of ripples,

retorts
that became
a distortion
of lip,
a thought unarticulated,

a consciousness
as a horizon
more knowing
than yourself.

tin-tinn-ambling 03

you spoke
as if untrained
in the power
of your voice,
hesitantly hushed.

but then
you laughed,
a bell
escaping its iron

by some, sudden
too powerful, swing
cast off to form
an unending exponential
curves
upon my ear, the air
a sound that climbed
my spine
as if is was
a staircase;
stuttering on each
aged, overused step.

but I could not
resent you,
for it was
the upward, awkward
avalanche
of a child's footfall
somehow always eager
to leave the last
step behind
even if
ill balanced
upon the next.

lightning 03

I am walking
between the
lightning strikes
trying to
giving my mother
another chance
to undo me,
to take me back.

and a pink strip
of cloud,
a tear within sky
is opening to me
flickering, the promise
of a universe beginning;

even as I attempt
to use this terror
as a crude reset
to this wound down watch
of a heart beat.

but these thoughts
are as known to me
as my fingerprints,
as are all the things
that left all the other
lines in my skin.

and I want to
scorch them away
with lightning.

leaning   03

the slump,
  the asymmetrical form;
    the surrender.

        a hand upon a rail,
         a fist upon a cane.
          the arch of a back
            in release
            or relent.

              a stumbled foot,
               a refusal to fall.

                  a prayer to end
                   all need for prayers
                     or
                       just the sun seducing
                       another
                         into wordlessness.

                    the intent
                     of the angle
                       of a leaning man.

evidence 03

her pulse twitched
to the frantic rolling
of her eyes,
as her teeth
pushed back her lips
into an unnatural smile
trying to escape
her skull
to be feral again.

but it was the
edge of her words
that drew blood.

all the hissing s's
and spitting t's
of wounded
swears, curses
and growls,

committing all the crimes
her ferocity
clenched hands
wanted but
could not help
curling
unsatisfied
with carving at
the palms of her hands.

as if there was
still too much space there
for her prey
to breathe.

but not quite
a victim
she felt violated
by the lack of bruises,

that somehow
only lacerations

were listened to.

that no one understood
that threats
were promises
not proposals

and in the mind
they really happen,
even when the events
do not.

she clasped
her fingers to her
own throat.

just for evidence…

stalking 03

I want no more
hands upon me;
no more
expectant eyes

and all other
parts
that assume
rights to me.

I sit
and imagine if
I hold myself
quietly enough
I will become
as a tree

with the patience
to root myself
so tenaciously
and seed
so hopefully.

but I am
a biped
and in such walking
comes running.

and the judgment
I cast upon
those eyes
ravenous upon my ass

with the slam of a door.

you'd think I
was in tall savannah grasses
with such stalking.

disarming 03

your distress attracted me
and I waited
for weakness
with a horrible patience.

a pulse you do not
detect,
a breathing you
suspect
but cannot verify.
voice,
a branch splintering
at every bend
and fades back
into the corners
of the room

drowning
in the crashing waves
of a thunderous silence
with intercepting turns
arches as frozen tides
curling upon each
other.

I am obvious
in the one sense
that you refuse.
that corner eye
shadow
fading into your reverie,
fractured small stills
between your chords;
decipherable
directly upon the ear,
felt upon the throat
and unclasped
all else with its
disarming.

and then start

a shiver
that I could
have come and gone
without your notice.

the missing 03

patient as sun
you hid a dark
behind your brilliance

so I would have
a light to read by.

everywhere
I was the blur
of a face desiring
you
in the longer seconds
of a street corner
when, above all voices,
you laughed
like brass;
a force that altered
the flight, the arch
of birds

and the trajectory
of the clumsy shapes
of my words
and scattered
my most well begun
intentions.

I know only
that now my dictionary
has a torn page
reminding me
of the missing.

rapt 03

you extended
your self
so readily
separating
your skin
from your bone.

wrapped
around my shoulders,
a place to curl
offering tears
as a source of water,
a salt lake
nourishing my tongue
with its memory
of sand,
of fathoms

and captured me
in your each breath,
lacerating the air
with your sigh
and all it implied.

a tired release
an expelled worry;
a recollection
enveloping you in
resurrected flesh,

just to make
more room for me
or
to pull me closer.

that your mercy
was really an
unadmitted love.

gestalt 03

shifting like a fractal
ever extending
but the same pattern,

the first to know it,
the first to deny it,

you smiled
at a yet translated
amusement
that was about
to be invented upon
my lips.

you could have spoken it
but you always waited for me.

as if you could   skip
two neurons ahead
traversing a wall
that became a veil
upon your lifting it.

slipping through
my hands
shaping into
whatever pleased
me
whatever eased
the obligation
in my eyes.

a Rorschach
to my every expression.
an unashamed laugh
upon the sky.

salt 03

tenderly
extract & separate
thin film,
this flesh,
vein by vein
from the pulse
trapped within it;
the life wriggling
within a
knotted net.

I am gutted
a fish split ,flayed
and fluttering
a meal for
desperate
net-ravaged hands
even as I gasp
terror,
a choking scream
at the center
of the cerebellum
radiating, repeating
a last signal.

survive.

I am drowning
in this desert,
this place
with out an ocean.
only that salt
will save me.

terminal 03

intelligence
as an
emotional disorder,

eyes
from the other side
of a thousand years,
arched with an ache
of knowing,
of seeing;
of reflections
that cascade upon
the invisibility
of the air.
they gaze through me
and though they
seemed so focused
upon their own nearness,
it was a distance
they searched.

lips
arched, cracked, bleeding
into a smile
that knew
that in the distance
there was no horizon.
they were about
to say "never"
but never
did so.

that all things die.
how anything small
ever touches
the infinite.

dead-ringer 03

blue before morning,
black veins upon the sky,
the expression
of a barely audible face.

bare branches
expulsed from earth
like exposed nerves;

a fear bound tree
my voice,
a butchered gray.
I listen to only
the dead or the dying.
the living
have too many reasons
to lie.

the shaded whispers
the mute lo-fi echo
scratching in some
prematurely buried box.

a bell,
my dead-ringer.

the truth
comes from
a lying place
and a constellation
mimics
my configuration
through some
reverse astrology.

I control the stars tonight.

they gather at my feet,
children for a story,
begging upon my brow,
a misplace halo.

I must admit
I want you
as close
and as
consistent.

the drowning 03

but always spinning
in a weightless darkness,

and I see you
a sunrise across
the ocean.
my skin desperate
to absorb
the little warmth
that has the fingers
to reach for me

but the tide
glides
between my toes
reminding me of depths
I must cross,
I must swim
or drown in
to reach you.

my eyes,
aching orbs
of longing,
my lips,
fear.
my breathing,
an excuse
to keep me from you.

the salt
that my tongue thirsts
for,
the drunkenness
of ocean
depths and desert.

there are firsts
I want seconds of
and sleep now
comes easier.
my arms open,
it is a worm that
slips over
and I slip into.

this is an obituary
to live by,
the unmournful drowning
of myself.

risen 03

doused
but evaporated
naked
by the sun,
a drought has forced
me up.

remembering
the ocean
like a ripple
in a stone,
a fossil
to all that lived.

water
a drapery,
a garment
with no fiber
or printed finger
to mark me.

and in this sun
my shadow walks
before me
like a premonition
to the sand
to prepare
for my footfall.
my breath articulates
itself
with a language
it has for all ears
but mine.
speaking
of the air
it needs
and the scent
it is searching for.

glisten 04

between the fingers
at either end of
a weak smile,

a silken cord
that stretched and thinned
behind your
closed
exhaustion enlightened
eyes
until
only its glisten
held it by
the ends,

an infinity
of line

as long as light
would hold;
as long as the sun
still had
the mind
to reflect off
even the
smallest of things,

.

you would hold
onto what
your fingers
could not.
onto what other
fingers
thought so easily
to take.

and the morning
shown
upon a prayer
that had no god
but you.

keichu's wheel 04

what is a wheel
without a center,
spokes
without an axis?
the members
are the structure,
the structure
its own dynamic.

a void
that creates
the surface,
sculpture in the round
with no way around
it.

and even in this ---
a point of density.

upon me now,
pressing through
just short of puncture.

my breath relents
and a star shifts
from orange to red
and a signal
is the static heartbeat
that metal ears turn to.

god is
anonymous and never
the same one:

the gravity of a planet
holding a black skin
taut around a corner.

a black hole
drawing
our awe
and
our voices
into silence.

my hand now.

tendrils & tendons
suddenly crucial
suddenly strained

collapses hinge upon it.
(though collapse
would just be
another structure)

I do not have the right
to compromise.

a sobbing moment
rattling around
in this rotting shell,

it MUST be me
who stands here now.
even if I never understand

something needs me.

even if I do not need
myself.

primitive 04

and I am awake,
with the shapes
of tortoise shells
and soccer balls.

and galaxies
dancing
toe to tip of finger,
sewing the seams
of all five sides;

that this just may be
a carved out infinity

or that
civilization may
just have accidentally
occurred
in the microcosm
of a spore.

that ancients
understood more
than us
with their turtle backs
and
childish imagings;
their still more
beautiful
sense of alone.

am I

an atheist
counting on a god
where my life will fail.
or
an agnostic
secretly smiling, already,
upon the answer?

or is this empty
just another cathedral
that will amplify
my echo?

these thoughts
hover and fly over
like the dimly lit
cement overpasses
that in this moon
look ancient
and
forgotten,

(in my more
primitive imaginings)

unchanging 04

what would I be

if I loved
someone who said
that I
should die or
should not exist.

that I
should have
gratitude, affection
or even
arousal
for anyone
who said
that.

anyone

who believes this
the way
that most of us
learn the horizon
and
believed it to be
the border of the
universe.

a falsity
our intellects know
but
our daily eyes
still pray to.

what are you telling
me

when your every act
is directed
by the lines of my face
and
the curve of my hip

and not by
the wanting of my eyes,

that I am nothing
but my mirror's
reflection
and if it is not
brilliant

then
nothing at all.

what would we be
with all this unchanging

than
the silence
we are now.

deluge 04

I have fins
and other
nameless anatomies
reaching the walls

holding me
to a floating place
in this room

and this figure
sways
the drunken,
muted
screams of
ocean

even as
a deluge is
coming

in such a world
I will evolve
and breathe

finally.

and the sun
will have
a crystal

to worship it
in every wave

in every blessed
drowning
of all the
mistaken words

I would have
to describe
this.

balancing 04

my finger lines it,
the shallow
the shine.

I am
rough and bloated,
a demon
with charging eyes.
a bolting
made into a bolt,
and then
into thunder

a jagged that
cuts cleanly
with it's
unforgiving
power trampling
the green grass
it
grew from.

but the green
is patient,

it will grow
from me soon enough.

just like all of
our rages
eventually sound
like the hands
that slapped us
as children

and all of our toxins
cure us
of ever loving them
again.

balance
is not about beauty,

it is
as clumsy
and haphazard
as our choices
and
as undeserving
as our consequences,

but it always comes.

blessed 04

blessed
with all that is
a burden,

I am sane
enough to scream,
fertile
enough to bury myself.

a want of grieving
outwardly,
a wailing widow,
a devastated child,

in me
must be
the straight line
of my mouth
and the gleam
that gives no light
to my eyes

but only
illuminates my skin
pale with its both
knowing and disbelief

that these things
just can't be.
but are.

I pray upward
to an empty sky
that is peering into me
for answers
or at least
a vessel
to store itself within.

this clarity of star
and
unpronounced wind
wants me,
a lung for its breathing

even as I   hesitate
in the purpose of it.

and my throat
is too trafficked
with words
unlistened.

I am.
I am alive.

but it is
the temptation
of all things
to become
its other.

dry heave 04

my jaw clenches
down upon
the air hardening
upon my throat.

it is a breath
I cannot swallow.
a rape, a lie.
I cannot allow

why have I
been handed this?

I am parted,
departed
and
petitioned

a scream that is
scattered
with too many targets,
a systematic fracture
that leaves me
with out surface.

pain without grief,
grief without name.

unsettled within
my stomach,
it sits behind
my eyes
diffused
beyond recollection.
but a growth
spreading my ribs
into continued
breathing,

I have somehow existed
beyond the universe's
intention
but still my fingerprints
are on nothing.

clearly 04

suffering becomes a
surface of its own,

with its own
horizon
at invisible angles
to all others

unvisible
but not
unnecessary.

it's intimacy
with wounds
is an act
of lovemaking.

and loss,
the distant cry of a bird
and a sun rising.
my skin
ravenously feeding
upon its heat.

a heartbeat
from behind
an eardrum
counting out
my vulnerabilities

and my breath
thanking them.

for this
barren place
to see myself

clearly.

outside 04

outside the sun
as all cold things
are,

no god has the right
to love me.

it has left me
outside
its skin.
reduced to flesh,
to a sin
it created
to demean me
with.

I was born
to die..

a fertilizer
to produce or bury.

earth
wants no gods nor devils

it is best not
to play chess
with megalomaniacs.

fossil 04

patience
is the only holding
upon my tongue,
a taut muscle
in all it has learned:

the futility of its
shapes upon
the air,
it curves, a clay
that will have
no eyes upon it.

just a horizon
of mouth,
and a stare;
a sky's absence of moon,

a line that
dreams of mountains,
even as mountains
crave valleys.

I wish my pulse
would know either

I gaze unrelented,
for all other heartbeats
have aligned
to this same
hypnotism
and the mechanical
is the last
function.

I am a fossil
a concave
left by the living
surrounded by
the immovable

intangible 04

"are you bored of me yet?"
she feigned indifference
behind the drooping lids
drunk with the weight
of the security
in his answer.

"no . . . not
yet"

his words
tried to create a
jealous doubt
that his gaze immediately
dissipated
with its unblinking,
its unyielding.

it was meant really
to do that anyway. . .

"are you disappointed in me
yet?"

"no
but you keep trying,
you have to mess up
eventually. . ."

that somehow saying
it was perfect
would make be less so
or
make it have to be
all the time.

a gold leaf page
that had both
its own flight
and its own shimmering,
that single breath
or
uncareful hand
could crumble.

they knew better
than to touch
the intangible.

saddicted 04

my eyes
scratch my eyelids
with all this tired.

but I am
addicted
to the epiphany
that desperate nights
and
suicidal highway commutes
lead to

the numb that
frightens me,
the speeds
I am unafraid of,

all the murders
I imagine
and
never commit.

because
just admitting this
might just hurt
someone's
sense of belief,
a lie that
is suckled upon
until it offers
no milk

then it
is just
a lie
again.

pause 04

a human being
looking straight into
a nuclear blast.

ego-full simian eyes
and
primate mind
finally able to value
the position
of a single atom

and exactly what
it means
at a 50 mile radius.

a realized transience,
an obvious fragility,

a pause between
reflex and reflection.

a fear that only
forethought
can see against
the inevitable
line of the horizon,

a silhouette
indistinguishable
from its shadow,

why riots
break on the quietest days
and
atrocity
has a mother's hands

in death
nature seems to
remember us.

invisible things 04

all life is
inferred, imagined, or invented.

walking
I am letting
such empties
fill me.

what if all the oxygen
just ran out

just now.

will I know then
just how much
invisible things matter?

in passing cars
I am looking for
all the affections
I cannot feel now.
all the unrequited,
all the faces
I gave to them.

just looking for
something to miss,

so that these
forced sighs
would have a reason.

as common sense
is sold in store fronts
as something novel,
I whisper "hello" to
passing mouths
that timidly
shape the word
back to me.

if they look at all.

as if sound would
tether and tie,
as if voice was
a promise.

but I am really
just counting all the ways
I don't really matter.

my bones will not last
as long as these brick-faces
but they will outlive flowers,

as if there are
correlations
between time and beauty
that we have yet to know.

but my only thoughts
are for
midsummer crickets
and jasmine.

writer's block   04

my windshield wipers
run off anxiety
as my pen
conspires to be out of reach
to make me a smoldering
hump of debris.

writer's block.

in this rain
flowers are drowning
in their reflections

and I have released
all my best words
in too early a season.

though the sky is
offering rhythms,
well threaded screams
and
offbeat interruptions

and silenced coughed.

the next breath 04

and there were jubilant giggles
that made your knuckles
white with all the blood lost
from them.
from the tension
that was your only sense
of equilibrium.

you sighed
a wanting that
may never have
an upsurge
as surfacing,
a reflection
that dared not
look upon itself.

and you scrawled
as with a child's pen
a rageful alphabet
with your fingernails
upon your too
unscarred skin.

there was a tide
that your throat
was gurgling upon
an instinctive habit
you wished would fail.

why could you
not have mercy for
yourself.
you were incapable
of surrender
in any form.
and earth was calling
through you,
weeding you out

or was it that you knew
that all you needed
endangered
all you wanted.

which was really
more important?

the answer
would decide
the next or the last
breath.

debris 04

it was a silence
that suddenly
had a shattering
beneath my feet.

I was stepping
upon debris again.

I disrobed
and searched myself
for symptoms,
the sores that would open
hungrily
mouths of newborns
tasting the smell of
my desperation
upon my breath.
I was gasping for
whatever oxygen
this claustrophobic night
had left me
and my wounds
refused to reveal themselves
red
yet still ached with
infection

how can the unseen
be so open.

soft 04

"your hands
are soft"

and that is
all that matters.
how I feel

to you.

I sit,
a fracture,
a barely breathing.
a glowing heat
dragged within
my flesh
that is dimming.

oh,
but I have
good skin.

it's just the
rest of me
that isn't good

enough.
enough.

even your concern
is a form
of selfishness;
a child's whimper
begging mother
to stop scaring you
with my all too
human
reddened
thought-flooded eyes

beggin me to
put things
back neatly
on their separate
shelves and
never touch
them to each other
again.

a salt water and acid
harmless
but explosive
on contact.

soft.

I'll have to take
your word for it

my hands are forbidden
to know my own skin.

gestures   04

you splayed
your hands,
two Chinese fans,
then allowed them
to greet each other
first tips,
then root,
then slowly upon the wrists.

the texture
of your skin assuaged you
with its reality;
the motion,
a thing to do
at a moment
of immobility,

gestures that
assured
that not all
sensations
would eventually
numb you.

but had
a warmth
and subtle texture

to keep you feeling.

ambush 04

(and in your presence)
the sky was fighting me
for my breaths
dragging them out of me
as a tether
toward you.

and in the night
I felt what
the blackness must;
stars as a small rain
reminding my skin
of its each living part
its every reactive surface

respond only to you.

and even the
wet pavement with its
unnamable objects
and chemical debris
had the perfume
of a memory

of me,
of a must have been
          in this celestial ambush

of eyes like mine
          glimmering with grateful confusion.

unuseable 04

I am maddened as a god
catatonic and impotent
at the knowing
of the power
now shaping
the lines
of my fingertips,

the marks
I leave mean nothing
in a world worshipping
the immaculate,

they're just washed away
by the maintenance crew.

go without a garbage man
for a day
and you will see
humanity's most profound
invention,

the unuseable.

delusions
are just horrible truths
etiquette
refuses us to say.

we would forgive
schizophrenics
if they would only
use the proper fork
for their word salad.

unseen 04

I sprawled,
sun soaked cat
on a powdered beach;
on the smallest
moving target at the edge
of a mundane galaxy,

my mind fogged
with comfort,
my feet
certain of the flat
beneath them

the line,
the span
of an uninterrupted blue

it reminds my eyes
of the parts
that stretch
where I cannot
and all the needs
that the curve
of my throat
cradles,

and that breath
is a blessing
invisible

and I now know
myself
by remembering
nothing,

scarless & endless,

even as my flesh
screams
of its
crevice & curvature.

an echo
dropped in a well,
forgetting that it can
float

I now see
the ripples
of an ocean
that has yet
to show itself.

beautiful lies 04

bubbles
fragile
and yet places
unto themselves,

sometimes beautiful places,

before groping hands
and probing penises
decide
your nothing but
a piece of pussy.

and will rupture
any place you are
just because . . .

I must be nice
to keep unruptured,

a place
that lets you think
you are god,

that lets you think
this is right,
a natural,
adaptation.

that is why
women whisper
around their daughters,

hoping that the lies
will last long enough
for the truth to catch up
with them,

with a thicker skin.

there is only one truth.
it all is lies.

quantified , qualified
and justified
with the fewest
bruises.

treadbare 04

the skin
of this soul
is worn.
all that
is touch
is ache
as much as it
is comfort.

treadbare
my nerves
are colliding
a concussion
from within,

my breath
pulling
upon my halo

like the inner curve
of a rose petal
sings,
the acoustics
the acuating
of every nervure
being strummed
in offhand
gestures,

releasing a pollen
thinking me
a place to copulate

third factor 04

only a human being
can see a rainbow.
the water,
the air,
the sun,
but it is our
myopic perception
of light, of spectrum.

it is what we don't see.
as much as
it is what we do see.

10111

and in this universe
of swarming agendas
to survive
that thrust forward
and receive their shape
from what
resists them:

at tree carved
by gravity and sky;

a galaxy
strung like a pearl
around a collapse;

a carbon
inviting four others.

an order enforcing,
a chaos disrupting.
leaving complexity,
life
as the scattering
of such collisions

from this
unaccounted for
transience,
a rainbow,
not of its parts
but beyond them.

"i am"

splaying as
a virus or a flower.

same old script 04

my fingers
dance
to my imaginings,
notes that
asphyxiate,
exasperate
me
with their
faint grasp
of how deliberately
gentle
I am being.

bruises
that were all
your excuses
I refused to accept

to swallow.

and I will never.

this terrible hungry horror,

you scream
that you have claws
but never show them.

even so
they would
never cut deeply
enough into me

as no part
of you
ever does.

you will never.

I close my eyes.
there is no reason
to watch
a performance
I've seen before.

forecasting 03

and the glowing
opinion-boxes
are telling me

all that I already
know that would
happen,
and pleasantly suggest
appropriatly
rehearsed
reactions.

the world rewritten
in every flicker.

I would learn more
from the dance
of a candle.

I look because
I am afraid not to
the millions fixating
upon these pigmented
shadows
upon the cave wall.

I only look
to see what they are
seeing
to read what "truth" the
world expects
from me.
so I can hide behind
what they expect

and so I might see the traces
that must have preceded
1918   1938   1953

how do you spot
the front
of an unforecasted storm?

acting up again 04

add a dis
to something
and it can be
undone
(or at least
rounded down)

disinherit,
discord,
disgrace,

and in these storms
I attempt
to camouflage
myself

and to
disappear

from my own worry.
(as if appearing
can be undone)

from this far too
tested and proven
hypothesis

of what just might
happen.

but I am still
expected
to act surprised.

a judgment
hurtling down from a height
unseen
and felt only
in its impact.

a pain
only balmed
with either
cruelty or kindness

one the most accurate
the other
the most rational

forgive me

I am a scar
over an old wound
that acts up
when it rains

third eye 04

creviced
and older still
than my hands,

a sun
whose surface
is leaving me.

Orion
is positioned
again
two stars
upon my eyes

and a third
of the implied
pineal

upon.
my forehead

and the voids
are holding
the sky in place
with their
appetites

the only way
to rid myself
is to go faster,

to escape
the pronunciation
of my name.

and the telephone poles
are caduceus
communicating
my fury
in the coldest
of codes.

I am completing
an arch
of that conduit

but I rumble
and lumber
through
the material

it is a sludge
that is suckling
upon my feet.

ache 04

and this ache
in my neck
is holding
up my head,

the necessities
rousing the drowsy
ape
that was dreaming
of larger things
than
small life.

my eyes
have gathered
too much wool
and
I intend
to collect more

until my sight
is refraction
and crystalline

and this ache
can no longer
obligate me.

no more
a suture
holding my eyes
to the sun,

I will choose
to see it
with my
enumerable skin,

and my eyelids
are a planetarium,

a cathedral
that has no god
than this long
silent sigh,

whose breath
may still be expanding
back
upon itself.

therapy 04

those words:

"and why is it
you feel that you
do not matter. . ."

that obligated
curiosity
that got you paid
by the hour.

eyes that had
no sympathy
or antipathy
but were scanning
over a daily schedule
that hung
before your gaze

invisible to me
except for the
side to side
motion
that never registered
anything I said.

I was supposed to
pencil in
a catharsis,
a scream,
a false orgasm
of insight
to make you feel
as if you were
doing well,

pretend I was
seduced
eluded, deluded
and the conclusion
of your clever
maneuvers.

you cared only to
hear a chant
worshipping a healer,

that your every miscalculation
was my pathology
my refusal
renounced.

so tell me
why is it
I feel
that I do not matter?

tangled 04

the only warmth
I hold
is the cup
in my hands.

my slow breaths
are hoping its heat
will burn
the lines
from my palm,

a scorched earth policy
translated
to chiromancy
that somehow
these lines
can be rewritten

or perhaps
untangled.

but they are knots
split, frayed and forked
with indecision
and wrung apart
with worry

and I wonder
if even my neurons
have been spun
into this same
discord.

the settling 04

I am surprised
not to see
glass smashed upon the floor,

that the storm
passed through
and left me
its only piece of debris;

that so much violence
could happen
in near silence

and then
so neatly fold up
like tomorrow's clothes.

I'll have to wear
the uniform again,

even after
I just tore everything
off me.

or shall I say

everything
that had attached itself
to me.

for now I will sit

and watch the
the upturned dust
settle back
into its old places.

constant 04

no one wants
to hear
that I hurt.

I am a universe
expecting mercy,
wanting a weak
moment
that my planets
will not tolerate.

so much
am I
hinged upon.

sun
that wishes to be moon
so that it may have
a shadow of earth
to hide in.

a gravity
that needs
to pull inside
itself
and see
to what constellations
it leads.

exhumation 04

"the world is a lie"

these words were implied
in all you taught me.
a shadow
that hung behind
your every expression
like night
behind the pink of morning
sky.

and it wasn't entirely
untrue,

the words.

and then something
broke.

an eruption
an ebullient glowing
of living form
woke
and its most
subtle,
unpronounced gesture,
just the force
of its life
rupturing
a dead husk
with a thousand
spiderous glowing fissures.

and I could hear
your breath again
as if holding it too long
as if once buried
and now exhumed.

your eyes darted
a terror of what
you felt within.
it was the only response
you had
for unrecognizable things.

you looked to
every corner of the room
pretending you heard
the shuffle
of a threatened approach,

but you backed away
from me

when my hands
only wanted
to pull back
the last piece
of hardening.

plague 04

and I am wondering
if
the box that Pandora
opened

was simply
a thought
followed by another,
followed just short
of a horrible conclusion

and that I have opened
just the same.

a last atrocity
simply contemplated,

leaving me
clasp handed
and
gasp breathed
in a terrified
psychological
immune response
of systematic
panic and distraction.

a hybrid
of Sybil and Cassandra
in my
fear and accuracy.
waiting for a
plague
in which all mothers
are carriers.

savanahhh! 04

she growled
low and guttural;
the sound
that makes
humans shivering primates
waiting for a tooth
but
her eyes
steadily piercing first

at the man
trying to tell her
that his brutality
was natural selection.

the man, now a boy
with his head
shrinking into his neck
and with monkey's eyes.

"you know what the
difference is
between you and me?"

her tongue
licking from her lips
the salty terror
she had extracted,

"... I actually know
what that translates into...":

and she laughed
with the crispness
of the sky.

unanswered 04

I am no more
important
to god
than

a cell
that does not become
an errant cancer,
an atom
that does not
stray into oblivion
and a
neural connection
whose job
is to know
what green is.

god is no more

aware of me
than that
but no less
grateful

thankful
in a thoughtless way

we pray and scream
to something
that may not even
have ears
or
a language

and can no more
speak to me
than I can
with a quark.

but all of us
have ears
and
prayers still
go unanswered.

I am not waiting
for a father that
never was
or
is never coming.

you tried to force
this on me,

which is nothing less
than rape.

even without bruises
on my thighs
doesn't mean
you aren't trying

it just means
you won't get caught.

unidentifiables 04

the nocturnal eye
that remembers,

mother is scratched
there
her name
upon every claw
and practiced tooth

as this is an almost
conception
that knows it will
have no birth
so it will never die.

but the chant continues
upon a heart beat
upon a harp
upon the hum
that never happened
upon a word.

it makes
me sleep
where every
facial feature
forces a ferocity.
from my teeth

I am continuing
in this wind,
my scent
upon a predators
nostrils
from 20 miles
as my voice
travels backward
barefooted years.

there are pearls
that are eyes,
that have known
only the sea,
its darkness.

there is a
sketch
upon a desert
of rocks
fingers reaching
for a sky,
a blue
to share its black
for a moon.

and I love the
fragrance of a flower
when I do not know it.
and the whispers
provide
better conversation
and they never leave,

such sweet unidentifiables.

untestified 04

this blanket
consciousness
and a sleeping cigarette
has burnt
a hole in it,

and hasn't finished
the job yet.

a mind can be
strangled
by mortal hands.
and yours are trying.

and only make me
seem
a mad-woman
with assault-scorched eyes
milk-white with unwilling

no matter
the deep, the bleed or
the real.
of the penetration

and I am whispering
horrible truths
just to hear them
translated
in all the screams
I refuse to voice,

a rape
with a planet-full
of untestifying
witnesses
their eyes
sealed within their lids
like manic fireflies,

as hands
are upon my breasts
and a tongue
forced within my ear
a mindless beast
with the entirety
of it jaws and will
in me.

but its just toying with
a carcass now.

and my pen
is channeling
bell jars
sealing the echo
of a gun shot.

hide and seek 04

I accuse
my beautiful self
of the crimes
committed against
me.
a trace chased
still pursued,
still found
until I reached
a house of flowers
that upon my eye
immediately found
a direct bound peace
with me.
a relief,
a familiarity,
a finally, finally, finally.
here was the place
I wanted
behind all this
hide and seek.
cornered, curled, comforted
in a cloister of
ivy and trees.

found for me,
my not-so-beautiful self.
my could-have-been,
my should-have-been.

easter 04

it was
a small easter.
I sat
a realization
of an eggshell
of its own
fissures.

a carved out place
that catches a little
of all that falls.

an edge that all
tears upon
a corner where
the endangered curl
for shelter.

incision,
the inwardly reflecting
susurration,
a saturation
into the pressure
that has given me
this place to sleep,

this pinch of tugging.

the crisp
about to speak
pronouncement,
a clicking like a kiss,
reaching for me
with its sound,

pulling tendon
from tendril,

a gossamer
of old worship,
a gossip
of outgrown care.

a hatched
trembling.

absolute zero 04

light is a tunnel
into all things,

and I am
a remnant
trying to remember
the architecture
before the blast
before this shattering,

the ice lace
on the window
tells me all things
have an absolute
point
of stopping.

this chill
it creeps
to find a break within
my skin

and my stomach
reminds me
that there are
desperations

that must be
forever fed.

(well
not forever. . .)

dream : the last 04

we were women
in a room
of all ages

in this state of waiting.

each silence
had its own shelter
our lips, an escape

but in these last moments
we never used them.

we were waiting

for a decision
made without
our words.

an old woman
wringing her hands;
a child playing with
a corners debris;
an infant wriggles
with barely realized
sense of where
(even on such days
babies are born)

I sit

and the windows
are getting darker

but they will be brighter
soon enough.

just wait.

the skin of my face
is soft upon my hands
I am not cold or
uncomfortable
in any way.

in my arms
the newborn
kicks and glances
and
I feel and inner clock
stopping
and I cradle her
before the window.

we are fragrant
sighs
upon each other.

a bomb drops
and
a nuclear brilliance comes.

I tell her to wave hello.

relent 04

a line that
only infinity
knew the width of,

stripped
down bare
a vein
without a heart;
my thoughts,
a thread
without end
until cut
until tautness
of the weight
of two infinities
at both ends
makes the middle
relent.

a quiet devastation.

I must become
the emptiness
between
these
frayed ends.

a conduit
to conduct
that which will never
be
explained to me

but I must learn
to understand.

grace 04

in grace
I am nothing

that has not
already been spoken.

immaculately bruised
with your thunder
and threats;
I knew with all
your voices
at my back window

that any
of true power
would not be
so small.

it would not
even speak.

you called me
selfish
when all I really had
was a sense of
self

my hands were upon
my lap;
a patient shape
even as my leg twitched
in some rhythmic code
all that my mouth
was not allowed
to say.

for my throat
was too full
of the breath
you expected
me to hold.

dispossessed 04

do not love me,

I want nothing
to compare this to.

I do not want to know
what should have
happened

or to hear
the excuses
of
why it did not.

they only become
accusations
made by the guilty.

my hands
clench and want
such violent
justices
from me,

a hebephrenic
crone,
crackling static
warnings
on a street corner.
dispossessed by that
which houses me.

I rant truths
better undiscovered

and spit them upon
all who pass
too closely

I am a splintering
of folded hands
of cold discourse
of damnation.

almost 04

atrocity is
just behind my
fingertips
waiting
for the last
print to wear
down,

my last
identification.

it is only
a breath
that holds me
from this bite,

a pause
that retracts
all my poison
tips
for the few seconds
it requires
to change my mind

because that
is not a choice.
there is only
one.

and I hope
I never understand
the fear I have been
taught.

it is enough
that I
almost
act upon it.

common as rain 04

frayed hair
and
worry accosted eyes;
their language
more universal
than the one
waiting upon her tongue.

" the devil is a man's excuse"

her voice
scratched with smoke;
the cigarette
smoldering filtered glow
closely
threatening her fingers.
while the gold cross
in her other hand
dangled helplessly
as if for mercy..

she spoke
of familial tragedy
as if it was
as common
as rain.

but I would
understand the words
anyway
if only by the
shimmer of her stare,
the way
her shoulders
closed
as if against an
older crime
of unwanted opening,

that my question
had such
vivid shape.

all else
was subject
to erosion, corrosion
numbness and numerous
other age appropriate
responses.

the real 04

let there be light
a flint,
a flicker,
on a formation
a hologram
illuminated.

how many bits
of me
make the universe?

a scorched aurora,
a Kirlian sense
of self.
I extend beyond
what has been
cut from me,

but my skin
is an
expectation
of hard fingertips.

castoffs
all this, just the residue,
the precipitate,
of the real universe.

the sculptures scrap
upon the floor.

feeding upon each other
because it cannot
sustain
without the blood
of other creatures.

ash
on the periphery
of a glow,

matter
is the hell
cast from heaven.

fey 04

fey
you placed your
self -doubt
before my feet
for me to stumble upon

and enjoyed
the ruin of me
as a child
joyously scattering
a perfect field of butterflies
with your thoughtless
stomping
the stampede of
the enumerable
unfinished intentions

so directionless
and cutting
you were
through the tall grasses,

but upon the slightest
fading of my face

shattered upon
the air
and apologetically ,
as if a butterfly yourself,
fluttered
upon my sunlit hand.
saddening
your lips
for my disappointments,

even as you
carelessly dropped
me upon the floor.

half wound 04

the air,
a breath
of moon soaked night.

there are lights
and foot eroded cobblestones
ghostly
curling upon my inner ear
unbalancing me
with these quick coils
of young laughter
with their sense
of could have.

a reverberant strum
making a
cathedral echo
of my throat,
my temporal sense
is swimming
in an ocean,
a foam
unafraid to drown,

even wanting to.
even begging to.

my smile trembles
unsure
of what dance
I ask it to perform
so confusing
are such symphonies
of recalled non-existent
memory.

so hurtful to me
are such joys

I am stuttering
in this
like a child's
still half wound
toy.

the T 04

The doors close. too late now.
but then I have forgotten
how much I like the smell,
the way the trees run
when they're not really moving.

"the trees are running away,
 the trees are running away,
hi ho the derry oh the trees are running away.."

A childhood song.
The movement of the train reminds me
of when all things moved.
and never settled.
I survey the passengers,
always the same pattern of variation:

young lovers,
a family outing,
elderly couples,
giggling girls,
guys in baseball caps

and loners
busying themselves with cell phones,
notebooks
or the pattern floor.

grieving 04

dangling
from this
tired, unclosed
question,

like a child
on a rope swing.

comforting myself
with this motion,
this rocking
this reminded
remnant of mother.
it is a calm
well earned with
constructive cataclysm.

I turn my head,
open mouthed
and accepting the shapes
forming in the dark theater
of my eyelids

the one configuration
I cannot accept
is my own.

I am not this,
not what you see,
not what can be
done to me.

only in this
swaying
am I not an
over-reactive
immune response
to what so constantly
invades me.

do I recall
the last person I was
…in some vague
scent of summer.

grief releases
itself slowly,
in a series of pauses,
interrupted by
sudden memory.
and the realization
that such things
will never happen again.

then sobs,
then eventually quiet.

because no one is listening.

good night's insomnia 04

I haven't slept for 24 hours,but somehow I am
more rested and aware.
All the "walkers" are out diagnosed with high
blood pressure or high cholesterol or just trying
to beat a life-long curse of self hatred. and, or
course, I am being closely tailed by a coffee-
swilling 17-year-old in a rusted white caddy as I
scrawl broken, wandering words that ride the cir-
cular motion of my steering wheel as I precarious
steer with my wrist so I can write. Each pothole
creates it's own shorthand. You'd think I'd have
learned to steer with my knees
by now.
I walk into a DnD and I my morning eyes
note how a pair of sunglasses and a frantically
focused pen upon an anonymous 97 cent
notepad can make you intriguing to people who
would otherwise ignore you. They stare at me as
if they are expecting paparazzi. I order a
medium regular -- making it average to make it
easier for the counter people. $1.50. I give them
$2 and drop 50 cents into the tip cup while other
people pretend to be too hurried or too tired to
notice it.
A good night's insomnia. It balances out
the mind like a long feared trauma come and
passed; a fear that has already happened, leav-
ing you for once obliged to say and do absolutely
nothing because there nothing to do but stare
after it. Your eyes fixed to its stampeding back-
side because you know the moment you look
away a smallness will set in.The room is too
small and all minute threats that world made (to
keep you a good little consumer, a good little
worker ant)
have no grappling point on you.

not anymore.

Comets are small even then and you could almost
feel perfectly comfortable sunbathing in the gleam of
one as it plummeted to the ground zero of your
navel, you eyes marveling about colors of its dips
and trails --- the chemical traces upon the air.
"just like a sunset. . ."
as much an eventuality of nature.
the comedy of it strikes you even as you are in the
perspective of its tragedy.

The sun is rising above the trees now. Its heat re-
minds me of all the predictions I've heard about a
solar storm, a solar flare whose fingers reach earth
and strip her of her atmosphere leaving her children
naked and crisping in bare ultra-violet.
Like T.S. said: not a bang but a whimper
my evaluation changes on that one from day to day. I
think we're already in the middle of the whimper. (the
long slow wheeze of an old man expiring)
our arrogance, to think our end will bring such a
clamor.
(probably the reason we invented the bomb----
just to be damn sure of it)

I left a message at "walkers" again. (at 2:11AM to be
precise). It is a chat room for the depressed, bipolar
and otherwise "deselected" in society's survival se-
lection process.
I wrote the same humorless drivel that when I'm in it
always seems like despair but hours later just reads
like a stilted, contextually inappropriate soliloquy of a
walking caricature .
No one is more self-obsessed than the depressed. It
is the disease that herds smell on the ones they let
the lions have. A disease for only innately socially
minded monkeys pretending to be predators and
making their own into prey. As if they really could un-
derstand the wisdom and responsibility of instrumen-
tal aggression.

I guess such teeth
make atrocity easier to swallow.

I drive into the darkness, floating from a nearly completed
sobriety. Stumbling on the side of the road is a white shirt
and black pants dangling a black purse. Her face is a blur
of erratic motion.
"drunk" I think.
but then a second possible reality sets in and she is
injured, collapsing step by step into the mercilessly
exposing headlights of a the traffic of the backwoods roads
between these towns. Small places where noone sees their
neighbors because everyone works out of town.
quaintly uncaring
but I still don't stop.
"odds are she's wandering away from Damien's"
a bar frequented by harleys and old fords.
"besides she doesn't look injured.."
but I think to turn the car around and a new images comes
into focus. Me on the barrel end of a gun in a crack head's
hand.Yes, they even exist in suburbia but are much more
well hidden.
"sorry honey,...i can't even trust you.
I keep driving.
The assessment took seconds. humanity quantified; its
costs and benefits weighed with a cowardly bluntness that
betrays all that I tell myself that I am. a decision of coordi-
nated selfishness , but if I choose any differently and the
worst happens----the news and gossiping lips would say
that i had it coming.
"what was she thinking????"
one more assessment that would take seconds.
cast aside with clichés:
"trust is for suckers"
but trust is not an abstract ideal. It is a basic component of
sanity and mortality. There is no mastering it. It is not an ex-
pert skill. It is always a clumsy act. a trembling. it is simply
convincing yourself that the worst cannot happen to you.
and even if it did, there was no way you could have known
otherwise.even though you probably could have.

practiced denial is the core basis of socialization,
an ultimate misplaced trust.
just like the moths instinctively attracted to the
headlights of my car. before they had been floating in the
void, dimmed fluttering galaxies drifting in an
illusory calm,
a viscous silence, until they are illuminated by that which
will destroy them. a passing disaster too large for them to
comprehend or even see coming.
tonight, I am a force of nature to small things
oblivious to my capacity of oblivion.I swoop and swerve.
Each coming of a set of headlights makes this fog more
opaque with luminescence and I must simply trust the
next 3 feet of road.
"nothing is there .. and even if it is,
I couldn't have avoided it anyway"

i rely upon my believed precision, but all precise
 motions have an equally precise chaos following its own
ambitious elsewhere. as I am barreling through this night
with a
massacre of insects on my windshield.
trusting the road,
the sky holding me to earth,
a convenient pattern of missing, misaimed meteors,
a president's motivation.

an empty space you don't allow yourself to know you are
living in. Filled with your own projections and props that
you are convinced that someone else put there.
trusting the goodwill and favoritism of something
that may not exist.

trust is the act of breathing.
and that the next one is a choice
you should be making.

berceuse 04

a Celtic voice,
you sang,
as the rising moon
on a purple sky

your words
lilting the leaves
to a dervish dance,
lifting the layers
of dust
that had settled
between daily things

a waking chill
to my sun warmed body.
like the darkness
of starlit sky,
making me insecure
to my sense
of gravity.
my hair floating,
my finger flitting,
keeping time
to translucent shadows.

I danced in
daydreaming

orchestrating my smile,
manipulating my solitude
to bring you closer

as I threw myself
into adoration of you,
reliving, re-singing
my past songs of grief
and finding them
to be realizations.

but remembering
only dreams
and slumbering
whispers.

submerged 04

breathing,
the barely heard
sound of rising,
and resuscitating
aperture for night.

the intermittent pauses
in which your silence
spoke to me

a barely received
transmission
sent between breaths
translated
in most submerged
tide
lapping upon my feet

you existed only
in reflection
with no place in the sky;
found between
the many surfaces
of ocean.

dreaming
a bubble clasped
in the black depths
of sea.
sunk too far
below
the surface.

illume 04

you smiled,
your eyes
a polite distance
and invitation.
as I dodged
them
with artifice

and even though
this one sense
has failed,
all the others
detect you,

behind the night,

light bulb
luminescent egg
around which
all
my thoughts flutter.

just the nervousness
I need,

an awkward worship,
a backward candescence
you are absorbing
my heat from me
feeding this glow

even the molecules
of air,
the dust you have
disrupted,
it radiated

small universes
pulses
that burned as
furiously as suns

a star
collecting planets
in briefly exchanged
glances, dances
of should or shouldn't I
an orbit of adoration
that I know
will decays with time

but always leaves traces
of such mutual gravity.

cold stop 04

there is a doubt
nibbling on my wires.
trembling my hands
as I write.
it crosses each memory
with an ambiguous fear
and
I short circuit
into a jabbering
of unbelieved philosophies,
a rattling of corroded parts,

an empty that squeals
and screeches itself
in long drawn out drones.

all my mechanisms
are failing
form without function,
dynamic without direction.

which thread
of this
program
has my end
in its running ,

that the past focus
of any future eyes
may see
the strand
as deliberately followed.

but really
just row upon row
level upon level
of gears and levers

of closings, of openings
routing me.

and I smell friction
a burning
that eventually
leads to a cold stop.

cognoscente 04

the water danced
as you drank it,

a slow syrup
of articulated
consciousness.
a place of surface
with no edge,
you prayed to it
with the closing
of your eyes
and the worship
of your tongue
as it shaped itself
to a universe
it tried to swallow.

but the moment
you opened your mouth
and let the moon
upon it
it evaporated.

an essence
with its nectar;
in its passing,
a fragrance

even as you
breathed
to recapture it,
to relive a memory
that never happened
but should have.

and still could.

inlet 04

an echo
that caverns
have not the mercy
to forget.

an empty
that calls all others.

a vessel
the transient place
where voices
dwell, swell
and
find their last expression

and now
there's a
ringing in me
a water drop
sounding
the distance
to an outer night.

beyond the reach
fingerlet buried rivers
black burrowers
interrupting
my grey
with their clarity.
carved out tides,
tangled concavity
exploring itself.

a inlet
enclosing
an unnamed ocean.

esse 04

sEnse
  Sentience
  Sentence
sEen

kEn
  Skein
  Skin
hidE

  hiddEn
hideouS
 hide uS
  insidE us

  insIdious

origami 04

you folded
your napkin
with a ritual calming.

neat, cornered,
contained and ordered.

creasing the edges
with a slide
of thumb and forefinger
and then another,
and then another.

a placation,
a plication,
holding back
all complication
now striking their fists
upon your inner ear.

a pulse
of unacknowledged
wanting

that could be
buried in these fissures,
the valleys and mountains
of this origami.

shekinah 04

a universe
excommunicated
by ink,

a reality rewritten.

the moon
is a witch
riding upon
the clouds

a glimmer to hide
and a crescent
to direct me
a moan
in worship
of a blue.

mother is a planet

but you are
disemboweling me
with your theories
of hollow earth.

primitive eyes
with modern hands,
the mystery is dwelling
outstretched and naked
in a sleep
in the collective organism
of the soft light
of an autumn dawn.

but the mystics
are instead with
their concubines.
counting letters,
reading numbers.

seeking their names
in their translations
of god's sighs.

that answers
should always be
whores and mirrors.

disMANtle 04

a surgery
without an anesthetic,

an unerring cut
knowing where the vein is
the ache
of an open,
of a new empty,
the physician cannot
heal
that which he has
deliberately dissected.

so is the way
with intellectuals

"cogito ergo sum"

a voice I watch
flying over my larynx
as my own clung to
the bone
that created it.

the cartesian
reduces me to
spare parts.

an insightful system
of levers and pulleys.

i will slit my throat
to breathe, to speak
my mouth is too full
of the tongueless

the sweetest of salts
is the most quenching.
my resolve will spill,
dissolve
all pure white
surrounding
with its red.

"cogito sum"

quaking 04

my skin is shifting,
a continent drifting,
a tectonic plate
creeping,

soon my species
will no longer
recognize, resemble
each other
cast upon separate
islands.

a flint
of a long ago
fracture
layered upon
in buried shapes

a furtive threat
to fragile cities
a blossoming fault-line.
a weight
upon a sliver,
upon a point in me

all those reasons,
all these reliances,
to not move,
to shift or rumble
too quickly
.

on one
so unqualified
for such patience.

lusus naturae 04

you blinked
processing
my stunned expression
to your words
with a strapped, gagged
and autopsied
intelligence,

accustomed
to the cold
of the table
and the phosphor
of the lights
impaling you
in such exposure.

a restrained ravaging,
a completed question
waiting for its answer.

settling from a scream
whose timber
had splintered
my sanctuary
flitting in roof-beams;
a crazed swallow.

and left
a bubble
floating in my cranium;
air in the tip
of an egg.

a place
of inconvenient clarity.

a sun upon
my closeted eyes,
wincing.
unweathered skin
scorching.

illuminating
all mark and deformation,
all taxonomic failure.
the sinew of my legs
shivering with a foals
unuse,
a withered membrane
without a bone.

as if I could know
what was natural.

inertia 04

shadow of a tree
that has long been
cut down.
a haunting
forgotten of purpose
but has somehow
with a new one.

do all rhythms
degrade,
or will this one have
its own
inertia.

all this left
a pattern on me,
a melody cut short
finding
my incessant hum.
a chaos and imperfection
distracted
to a sudden sharp
or a falling flat
or a nerving natural

for a tone unvaried
eventually
becomes silence.

the panoramas passing
streak their fingertips
in last grip
upon my car window,

a gritty ocean
carving away at a shell
birthing both
destruction
and
unrepeatable beauty
upon the most
horrible claws,

my fingers
leaving fingerprints
on this aquarium
captured sky.

the rain,
a trail of stars,
the shape of an interference
against a black open
reminding me of
the sparkling,
the entry flames
of meteorites.

136

swat 04

I keep fleeing
the moment
just before

and I am an insect
struggling to turn over,
a fly
shrieking with my buzz
at a window.
my conceptions,
too unperceiving
to understand
glass

I only understand
that I do not
have the tools
to overcome it.

deselected,
eliminated
because I can not
adapt
to the impossible
to the contradictory.

fear
a fluid that mixes
with the blood
in my stomach;
each reactive
surface
a cold grasping
spine within me.
skin
my membranes
of inadequate defenses
behind glassiness
of my eyes,

a blocked moment.

a judgment
cast down
the castes,

the universe
had me destined
to be nothing
more
than fertilizer

when it put me
on the other side
of your hand.

life is a lesson
that eventually
kills you,
frees you.

bhurka 04

it always
comes down to us
placed at
barely intelligible distances,

a ghost
of threat
still hovering
in the air.

these histories
do not approve
what my dress reveals
and even less
of what it hides

cover all but my eyes
that you will not
look into.

a walking shame
a skin
that the male child
feared and suckled upon,
a slave
that a master
has bound
himself to.

a cord with a prisoner
at each end.

I know your deepest
fear,
it is the color
of my most
livid, lived
bruises.

I know your
lie,
that my skin
cannot exist
without injury
and that I need
your brutal hands
to protect me,

from your brutal hands.

Glaucon   04

this tolerated condition
and temporary
mask and mimicry,

we are just
monkeys
with addictive personalities.

humans are universes
that only collide
in mitosis,

in love
alternating between
drunkenness and withdrawal,

in disaster.

in death
just as primitive
and shrieking,

it's a photograph
this moment
this mind
a pantomime
shadows molding
their own forms
from the light
onto the wall.

arguing about
who is god.

self is a delicate denial
that melts
as waxl
upon a fingertip,

apes fascinated
with a fires flickering,
genius and atrocity
in the randomly
fortuitous misuse
of a tool.

too easily shaped
into something else

"they are strange prisoners"

bloom 04

and like a cloud
descending
every pore
devours your presence
as the grass does dew
in the desert.

even in such ravenous
greed
you do not
diminish
but expand

the kind of flower
the bees gather
around
just to look at,
and I am a bud
from branch
believing
I am
floating, flying, against the sky
suspended by my own will and unwillingness
to open

while you splayed
reciprocating
the sun.

jazz 04

my unsober eyes
keep postiioning the
triangles in the wallpaper
into the shape of a sail,

then stuttered alert
by a note sliding
gulping over the frets
the playful plodding
somewhere between a
christmas morning stampede
and
a new orlean's rain.

and my fingers
reciprocated
sliding the rail of my chair,
the sound seducing them
into caressing
anything within reach.

this drunkenness
is wearing off
and being replaced
with another

a slow repetition
a horn droning,
a bass stalling
a beauty emerging
from a practiced set
of finger positions.

"improvisational jazz,
imagine frank zappa
with ADD"

he shuffles guitars
while the saxophone
entertains itself with stray
notes
that dance like sunlight
worn,

a child in skipping reverie.

thaw 04

white
the most shivering
moon

my fingers
damming my eyes;
a glistening
trying to escape.

that you caught
breathing me in,
this winter
thawing in your lungs.
that i could be
even that close
to your heart.

the age of your voice,
the youth of your face,
the anger of
your helpless fingers

but the mercy
of your eyes
regarded me
with such an
inability to hurt.

you were holding
the wind from me,
the cold of
your dying.

glimmering in your
most worn.

an accustomed truth
at my aching throat
was still better
than the rape
of a lie.

legion 04

a consideration,
as distant
as the fading
lines in the wallpaper
patterning themselves
upon my glazed stare.

a happenstance
of meaning
while I'm sitting here
wondering, waiting
for that
inevitable appointment
still upon the corner
of my eye.

"I am alive now
I have eternity to die. . . "

these words
purchase another day
but i still hear it
infesting swarm
a plague
of chewing, chomping
fornicating, replicating
relentless locusts
puckering the walls
with their numbers,

destroying a years growth.

they are fat and fed upon
the warm corpse
of a host memory,
on my every neuron
dormant in a sea
of endorphins

until awake again.

www.ingramcontent.com/pod-product-compliance
Lightning Source LLC
Chambersburg PA
CBHW052104090426
42741CB00009B/1673